|| "Dedicated to all who seek to understand and appreciate Indian culture and tradition." ||

BENEATH THE SURFACE

UNCOVERING THE HIDDEN MEANINGS IN INDIA'S ANCIENT TEXTS AND LEGENDS

DR. JAGADEESH PILLAI

Contents

Contents

Prayer

"Om Asato Maa Sadgamaya, Tamaso Maa Jyotir Gamaya, Mrityor Maa Amritam Gamaya, Om Shantih, Shantih, Shantih"

The true meaning of this mantra is: OM guide me from the unreal to the real, from darkness to light, and from mortality to immortality.
OM Peace, Peace, Peace.

᭡᭡᭡

About The Author

Dr. Jagadeesh Pillai is a renowned Guinness World Record holder, writer, and researcher hailing from Varanasi, also known as the abode of Lord Shiva. With a Ph.D. in Vedic Science and a range of creative ideas and achievements, he is a true polymath. He is the author of more than 100 books including Research Publications. Although his roots can be traced back to Kerala, the people of Varanasi hold him in high regard and affectionately consider him one of their own.

Dr. Pillai has achieved four Guinness World Records in the following subjects:

"Script to Screen" - In this record, Dr. Pillai produced and directed an animation film within the shortest time possible, breaking the previous record set by Canadians. He has also received numerous national and international awards and recognitions for this achievement.

Longest Line of Postcards - For this record, Dr. Pillai created a line of 16,300 postcards on the occasion of the 163rd anniversary of Indian Postal Day. The event also included a questionnaire about the Indian flag.

Largest Poster Awareness Campaign - Dr. Pillai designed an awareness campaign on the subject of "Beti Bachao - Beti Padhao" (Save the Girl Child - Educate the Girl Child) to achieve this record.

Largest Envelope - In tribute to the Indian Prime Minister's

"Make in India" initiative, Dr. Pillai created a 4000 square meter envelope using waste paper to achieve this record.

Attempted - **70000 Candles on a 210 kg Cake** - To celebrate the 70th Indian Independence Day, Dr. Pillai attempted to light 70,000 candles on a 210 kg cake, which was recorded in World Records India.

Attempted - **Documentary on Dhamek Stupa of Sarnath in 17 Languages** - Dr. Pillai attempted to create a documentary on the Dhamek Stupa of Sarnath, dubbing it in 17 different languages. The result of this attempt is currently awaiting confirmation from the Guinness World Records.

Dr. Pillai is skilled in teaching the Bhagavad Gita, a Hindu scripture, and is popular among young people. He has helped many young people improve their lives through his motivational teachings.

In addition to teaching, he has composed and sung numerous Sanskrit Bhajans and patriotic songs.

He has also written and directed several short films and documentaries for awareness campaigns, and has volunteered with the police in both UP and Kerala to spread awareness about various issues through videos and photography.

Incredibly, he has produced and directed over 100 documentaries about the city of Varanasi, all on his own.

He has also helped and guided more than 25 boys and girls to achieve world records through creative and innovative methods. He is a multifaceted person who uses his intellect and the blessings given to him by God to excel in various areas. He is both a teacher and a student, always learning and teaching, and is able to master any subject he comes across.

He is a selfless social activist and motivational speaker who has overcome struggles and failures to become a successful and enthusiastic individual with a rich life experience.

In addition to his work with the Bhagavad Gita, he is also an efficient Tarot card reader, Astro-Vastu consultant, and a talented singer and composer. He has sung the entire Ram Charita Manas and Bhagavad Gita in his own compositions, and has sung the phrase "Lokah Samastha Sukhino Bhavantu" in 50 different languages. He is currently working on a detailed and scientific study of Vedas, Upanishads, Puranas, and the Bhagavad Gita. He has also composed and sung the Hanuman Chalisa and Gayatri Mantra in 108 and 1008 different compositions, respectively.

Awards - Four Times Guinness World Records, Winner of Mahatma Gandhi Vishwa Shanti Puraskar, Mahatma Gandhi Global Peace Ambassador, Kashi Ratna Award, Dr. APJ Abdul Kalam Motivational Person of the Year 2017, Mother Teresa Award, Indira Gandhi Priyadarshini Award, Bharat Vikas Ratna Award, Udyog Ratna Award, Vigyan Prasar Award, Poorvanchal Ratn Samman.

 providenza

Preface

India's ancient texts and legends have captivated the minds of scholars, mystics, and seekers of knowledge for centuries. From the Vedas to the Mahabharata, these works contain a wealth of wisdom, insight, and inspiration that is still relevant to us today. However, beneath the surface of these texts lie hidden meanings and interpretations that are often overlooked or misunderstood.

In "Beneath the Surface: Uncovering the Hidden Meanings in India's Ancient Texts and Legends," we delve into the depths of these ancient works to uncover the deeper layers of meaning they contain. Through a combination of historical, cultural, and spiritual analysis, we explore the stories, symbols, and teachings that have shaped Indian civilization for thousands of years.

With the help of experts in the field, we delve into the hidden meanings of some of the most well-known and beloved texts and legends of India, such as the Upanishads, the Bhagavad Gita, and the Ramayana. Along the way, we also examine lesser-known works, such as the Panchatantra, the Jataka Tales, and the Puranas, to gain a broader understanding of the rich tapestry of Indian literature and culture.

Whether you are a student of Indian history and culture, a seeker of spiritual wisdom, or simply someone with a passion for exploring the hidden meanings of ancient texts, "Beneath the Surface" offers a unique and thought-provoking journey into the heart of India's ancient wisdom.

This book will help readers to gain a deeper understanding and appreciation of India's ancient texts and legends, and the rich cultural heritage they embody.

The book is not only for those who are interested in Indian culture, but also for anyone looking for a deeper understanding of their own cultural heritage. The wisdom of ancient texts can be applied to modern lives. As we unravel the hidden meanings in these texts, we can gain valuable insights into the human condition and gain a deeper understanding of our place in the world.

We hope you will join us on this journey of discovery as we uncover the hidden meanings in India's ancient texts and legends. The knowledge and wisdom contained within these works can be transformative, and we believe that by studying them, we can gain a deeper understanding of ourselves and the world around us.

ᐖᐖᐖ

ONE

INTRODUCTION TO INDIA'S ANCIENT TEXTS AND LEGENDS

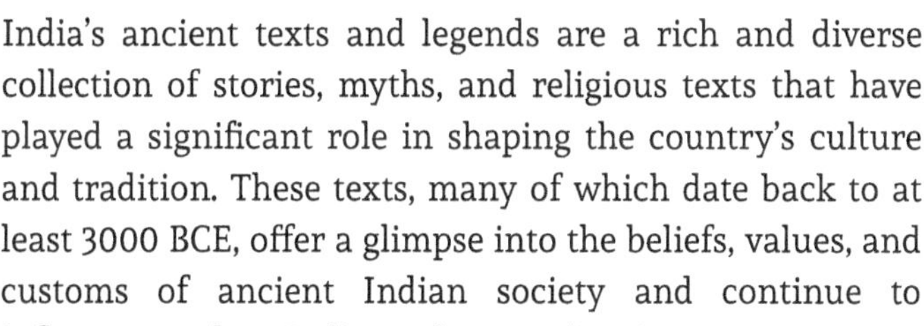

India's ancient texts and legends are a rich and diverse collection of stories, myths, and religious texts that have played a significant role in shaping the country's culture and tradition. These texts, many of which date back to at least 3000 BCE, offer a glimpse into the beliefs, values, and customs of ancient Indian society and continue to influence modern Indian culture and society.

One of the most significant ancient texts in India is the Vedas. These texts, which are believed to have been written between 1500 and 1000 BCE, contain hymns, prayers, and rituals that formed the foundation of the Hindu religion. The Vedas are considered to be the oldest sacred texts in India and are still studied and revered by Hindus today.

Another important ancient text is the Mahabharata, which is considered to be one of the longest epic poems in the world. The Mahabharata is a complex and multi-layered story that tells of a great war between two branches of a royal family and the consequences of that war. The story is filled with moral and ethical teachings, as well as lessons on the nature of good and evil.

The Ramayana is another ancient Indian epic that is widely read and studied. The story tells the tale of Prince Rama, who must rescue his wife Sita from the demon king, Ravana. The Ramayana is considered to be one of the greatest works of Indian literature and is still widely read and performed in India today.

In addition to these texts, there are also many ancient legends and folktales that are an important part of Indian culture. These stories, which were passed down orally through generations, often depict the lives and deeds of gods, goddesses, kings, and heroes. They often serve to teach moral lessons and provide insight into the beliefs and values of ancient Indian society.

The significance of these stories and their meanings can be seen in the way they continue to shape and influence Indian culture today. The stories and characters from these texts are still celebrated in festivals and ceremonies, and they continue to inspire art, literature, and film. The moral and ethical teachings from these stories are also still relevant and applicable in the modern world.

India's ancient texts and legends are a treasure trove of

stories, myths, and religious texts that have played a significant role in shaping the country's culture and tradition. These texts, many of which date back to at least 3000 BCE, offer a glimpse into the beliefs, values, and customs of ancient Indian society and continue to influence modern Indian culture and society. The moral and ethical teachings from these stories are also still relevant and applicable in the modern world. They are a window to the past and a way to understand the roots of Indian culture and tradition.

"India is the cradle of the human race, the birthplace of human speech, the mother of history, the grandmother of legend, and the great grandmother of tradition." - Mark Twain

TWO

DECODING THE VEDAS: UNDERSTANDING THE SPIRITUAL TEACHINGS IN THE ANCIENT TEXTS

An understanding of spiritual teachings in ancient texts, such as the Vedas, is essential for understanding the spiritual roots of many current religious practices. The Vedas are among the oldest known religious texts in the world; the originals date from the 8th century BCE and cover a range of topics from hymns to laws. The primary objective of the Vedic literature is to guide humanity towards the realization of their spiritual essence and the fulfilment of their life's purpose.

The essential teachings of the Vedas have been summarized as the three core principles of Dharma, Artha, and Karma. Dharma means living according to the laws or rules of one's religious or spiritual tradition. It includes adhering to the moral codes of behavior, observing rituals and studying the scriptures. Artha is the pursuit of material aspirations, such as wealth and prosperity, as well as the development of one's intellect and social standing. Finally, Karma is the belief that all actions have consequences; one's destiny is determined by the cumulative effect of one's actions, both good and bad.

These three teaching serve as the foundational principles of the Vedic religion and are frequently discussed in the ancient texts. The Vedas contain numerous hymns, incantations and ritual instructions to help individuals cultivate the strength of character needed to live according to these core values. They also provide a guide on how to attain the highest spiritual goals, as well as guidance on matters such as politics, economics, and social life.

The ancient texts of the Vedas are essential for understanding spiritual teachings. In composing these sacred works, the sages of India wanted to provide a moral compass and guide individuals on their spiritual journey. By following the three principles of Dharma, Artha, and Karma, individuals can begin to awaken their higher selves and explore their connection to the spiritual world. This will allow them to discover the true purpose of their lives and live in harmony with the divine.

ᗡᗡᗡ

"India is not a country, it is a continent." - Rabindranath Tagore

THREE

THE UPANISHADS: A DEEPER LOOK INTO THE SPIRITUAL PHILOSOPHY OF THE UPANISHADS

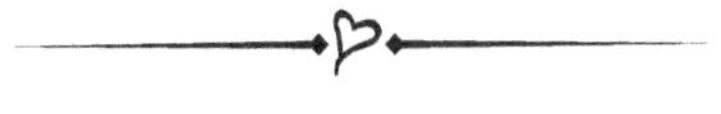

The Upanishads are a collection of ancient texts that form the basis of the spiritual philosophy of the Hindu religion. They are considered to be the foundation of Vedanta, one of the six schools of Indian philosophy. The Upanishads are also known as Vedanta, which means "the end of the Veda." They are considered to be the most important and influential of the Vedic texts, and they are still widely studied and revered today.

The Upanishads are written in the form of dialogues between teachers and students, and they explore a wide range of spiritual and philosophical themes. They discuss the nature of reality, the self, and the ultimate goal of human existence, which is to attain spiritual liberation and union with the divine.

One of the key concepts in the Upanishads is the idea of Brahman, the ultimate reality and the ultimate source of all things. Brahman is often described as the unchanging, eternal, and absolute reality that lies behind the world of appearances. The Upanishads teach that the ultimate goal of human existence is to realize the true nature of the self as being identical with Brahman.

Another important concept in the Upanishads is the idea of Atman, the individual self. The Upanishads teach that the individual self is not separate from the ultimate reality of Brahman, but is in fact identical to it. The Upanishads also discuss the idea of Karma, the law of cause and effect, which states that all actions have consequences and that these consequences determine the nature of future experiences.

The Upanishads also discuss the idea of Maya, the illusion of the world. They teach that the world as we experience it is not real and that our perceptions are illusory. The Upanishads also teach that the ultimate goal of human existence is to transcend this illusion and realize the true nature of reality.

The Upanishads are a collection of ancient texts that form the basis of the spiritual philosophy of the Hindu religion.

They are considered to be the foundation of Vedanta, one of the six schools of Indian philosophy. They explore a wide range of spiritual and philosophical themes, including the nature of reality, the self, and the ultimate goal of human existence. The Upanishads teach that the ultimate goal of human existence is to attain spiritual liberation and union with the divine, realized through the understanding of key concepts such as Brahman, Atman, Karma, and Maya. These texts still hold a great relevance and are studied and revered by many spiritual practitioners and philosophers today.

ᐅᐅᐅ

"The beauty of India is that it is a land of contrasts. It is not just one color, it is not just one smell, it is not just one tradition." - A.R. Rahman

FOUR

THE PURANAS: UNDERSTANDING THE DEEPER MEANINGS IN THESE ANCIENT TEXTS

In Hinduism, the Puranas are an enormous body of works, many of which are over 1000 years old and are of immense religious and cultural significance. They contain stories, descriptions of the gods and goddesses, stories of creation, and a vast collection of philosophical, social and historical material. Furthermore, they offer us insight into the deeper meanings behind the mythology, symbols, and symbols of Hinduism.

The Puranas are highly symbolic and can be seen as compilations of the many ancient ideas and philosophies that were used by Indians in the pre-modern era. For example, the Puranas contain many stories which involve the great gods and goddesses. These stories are not simply related to the divine and provide a way to understand the teachings of Hinduism. Symbolic identification of these gods and goddesses and their various qualities can provide insights into various aspects of life and the greater cosmos.

The Puranas also provide us with a deeper understanding of the innermost nature of humans. The Puranas teach us about the need for inner transformation and purification, and how to maintain spiritual balance. We can learn to identify the importance of karma, the cycle of life and death, the presence of good and evil, and other aspects which are integral to the teachings of Hinduism.

The Puranas also contain stories which have their roots in the Vedic traditions. These stories provide the moral values of Hinduism and can teach us about the importance of harmonious relationships, the necessity of humility, and the power of perseverance. They furthermore can help to provide a greater understanding of the nature of the divine, including the various representations of the various gods and goddesses and their interaction with the universe.

Finally, the Puranas also provide us with an understanding of the deeper metaphysical and spiritual aspects of life. For example, the idea of Brahman, the ultimate reality which serves as the spiritual foundation of all existence, is explored in depth through the stories. Furthermore, we can understand how to live in harmony with ourselves, the environment, and other beings through our religious understanding.

The Puranas provide us with a greater understanding of the symbolism, philosophy and history of Hinduism. By exploring the deeper meanings of these stories, we can begin to understand the basic tenets of Hinduism. Understanding the deeper meanings of the Puranas can help us to understand and practice our faith more fully and with deeper insight.

ϷϷϷ

"In India, I found a race of mortals living upon the Earth, but not adhering to it." - Ralph Waldo Emerson

FIVE

THE EPICS OF INDIA: UNCOVERING THE SPIRITUAL TEACHINGS IN THE RAMAYANA AND THE MAHABHARATA

The two epics of India, Ramayan and Mahabhart, are the stories of two great Princes, namely, the god and avatar Rama and the heroic Pandavas. They both contain spiritual teachings that have been used for centuries in India for guidance and knowledge about life.

The Ramayan is the oldest of the two Hindu epics and is said to have been written by the ancient seer, Valmiki. The story is that of a righteous king, Rama, as he embarks on a journey of self-discovery and understanding of the divine laws of karma and dharma. He encounters various difficulties and obstacles along the way, but ultimately wins the battle against an evil demon-king, Ravana. The spiritual teaching of the Ramayan is the importance of righteousness and devotion in order to find one's true purpose and connection with the divine.

The Mahabharata is the second of the two Hindu epics and is considered to be much more complex in its themes and teachings. The central theme of the Mahabharata is the battle between cousins, the Kauravas and the Pandavas, and is said to be the story of how order is restored from chaos and dharma, or righteousness, is revitalized on the Earth. Throughout the Mahabharata, spiritual teachings about duty, loyalty, and the consequences of our actions are expressed. The main lesson is the importance of following one's duty, even when it is difficult, in order to create a better world.

The Ramayan and Mahabharata contain numerous spiritual teachings and serve as sources of great wisdom and knowledge. With morality at the heart of both epics, they are examples of incredible stories that are still relevant in our present-day lives. The lessons expressed in both epics continue to influence and shape Hindu spiritual beliefs and traditions.

ᘏᘏᘏ

"India is the meeting place of the religions and among these Hinduism alone is by itself a vast and complex thing, not so much a religion as a great diversified and yet subtly unified mass of spiritual thought, realization and aspiration."
- Sri Aurobindo

SIX

THE BHAGAVAD GITA: A CLOSER LOOK AT THE SPIRITUAL TEACHINGS OF THE GITA

The Bhagavad Gita is one of the most inspiring and profound spiritual texts of India. The Gita is a verse scripture that is part of the great Hindu epic Mahabharata and is composed of 700 verses. The Gita is the bridge between the Vedas (Hindu scriptures) and the Upanishads (Hindu philosophy). It is considered one of the most comprehensive compendiums of spiritual teachings in the world.

The core teaching of the Gita is that a devotee should focus on the path of yoga, which encompasses faith, detachment, meditation, and selfless service. The Gita maintains that correct knowledge, correct action, and the relinquishment of desire are necessary components of the path to liberation. The Gita also sets forth a number of practical guidelines that a devotee should observe in order to harmonize the spiritual life.

The Gita directs the devotee to act upon the physical, mental and spiritual planes. On the physical plane, it emphasizes self-restraint and meditation. On the mental plane, it emphasizes the development of non-attachment to material objects and non-response to negative emotions such as anger and jealousy. On the spiritual plane, the Gita urges the devotee to surrender and accept the will of God. In other words, it recommends focusing on the Divine rather than on worldly achievements.

The Gita emphasizes the importance of non-violence, non-greed, non-attachment, humility, patience, and faith. It advocates performing one's duty without being attached to the fruits of labor and renouncing all material possessions. The Gita also extols the path of meditation and contemplation as a means of cultivating knowledge and spiritual power.

The teachings of the Gita can be summarized as "Knowing something and acting upon it yield success." By following the spiritual teachings of the Gita, a devotee can achieve his spiritual goal. The Gita stands out among other spiritual texts, as it offers practical solutions to the complex spiritual challenges faced by seekers in the modern world. The teachings of the Gita are timeless and offer faith, knowledge, and the way to spiritual liberation.

ᏀᏀᏀ

"India is a land of ancient civilization and culture, where tradition and modernity coexist in perfect harmony." - Dalai Lama

SEVEN

The Yoga Sutras of Patanjali: Understanding the Spiritual Philosophy of Yoga

The Yoga Sutras of Patanjali, written between 400 BC and 200 AD, provide many key spiritual concepts of yoga - specifically, how to free one's self from suffering and achieve lasting peace. Patanjali, a renowned Indian scholar and the author of the text, structured it as a 196-sonnet style summary. Although there are only four main sections or "books," the Yoga Sutras incorporate eight limbs of life and practice as a path to spiritual liberation.

The first book, containing 55 sutras, is samadhi pada. It focuses on the practice of yoga, and explains that when one builds awareness of different layers of self, he is able to be liberated from mental distractions. This first book also covers six processes of spiritual awareness - samprajnata samadhi, savitarka samadhi, sananda samadhi, savicara samadhi, sasmita samadhi, and asamprajnata samadhi - and outlines the need for a sequence of practice and concentration in achieving liberation.

The second book of the Yoga Sutras, sadhana pada, contains articles such as the five kleshas (mental disturbances), vrittis (thought patterns), and gunas (three states of energy). They explain how one needs to accept and overcome sufferings, as well as cultivate clarity of thought and control of the mind to achieve liberation.

The third book, vibhuti pada, explains how one can anticipate and use the powers of yogic practice. This includes the use of supernatural powers, such as levitation and clairvoyance, as well as achieving self-realization and contentment.

Finally, the fourth book, kaivalya pada, deals with the "final" and complete state of liberation. It is replete with advice on how one can remain in a state of yoga, engage in realization, and even experience life without rebirth. To reach this final state, Patanjali advises that one must practice non attachment and practice non-identification.

The Yoga Sutras of Patanjali provide many spiritual

concepts of yoga, teaching practitioners on how to free one's self from suffering and achieve lasting peace. Through its four books, Patanjali explains the processes of spiritual awareness and provide advice on how one can achieve self-realization and liberation. The text is a comprehensive guide on yoga as a spiritual practice, and can still be applied to the lives of many people today.

ϡϡϡ

"India has a way of mesmerizing you, captivating you, and fascinating you. There's a magic to India that's hard to explain." - Anthony Bourdain

EIGHT

THE TALES OF THE PANCHATANTRA: UNDERSTANDING THE DEEPER MEANINGS IN THESE ANCIENT STORIES

The Panchatantra is an ancient Sanskrit collection of stories that has been shared and passed down through generations, eventually being translated into more than sixty languages throughout the world. Its stories have remained popular to this day, and while they may appear to be simple moral fables, they contain significant moral teachings, deeper meanings, and psychological truths that are just as pertinent and relevant today as they were thousands of years ago.

The most obvious moral lesson of the stories is the concept that no one should act rashly, or rush into decisions without carefully considering them and weighing their consequences first. This theme is repeatedly highlighted throughout the stories, with characters often making choices based on their passions or emotions which are later proven to be detrimental. In "The Lion and the Bull," for instance, the lion had the opportunity to kill the bull, but instead chose to display goodwill and mercy - an action that later saved his life. This is an example of living in accordance with the Dharma, or righteousness, which is a major concept in Hinduism.

Moreover, the Panchatantra explores the idea that wisdom and intelligence are just as important as strength and courage. Characters with both strength and wisdom often outwit their adversaries, as shown in "The Mongoose and the Farmer's Son." Here, the mongoose helped the farmer's son to save his crops from being destroyed by rats, displaying intelligence and wit to outwit their enemies. The use of cleverness and wisdom is also demonstrated in "The Brahmin and the Mongoose," where the mongoose used his wits to save the Brahmin from disaster.

At its core, the Panchatantra teaches us the importance of friendship, loyalty, and cooperation, suggesting that these are necessary for any endeavor to be successful. In "The Brahmin, the Tiger, and the Six Judges," the Brahmin used his friendship with the tiger to escape execution, while in "The Monkey, the Crocodile and the Dog," the monkey was saved because of his loyal friendship with the dog. This teaches us that even the most formidable adversary can be defeated if we have friends and supporters to stand by us.

The stories of the Panchatantra may appear simple on the surface, yet they contain valuable lessons about how to live morally and ethically, how to evaluate one's actions, and most importantly, how to cultivate relationships. The wisdom embedded within these stories should not be overlooked, as it can help us become better people both individually and in groups.

ppp

"India is a country of many languages and many religions, but it is also a country of many beautiful landscapes and many beautiful buildings." - Gustave Flaubert

NINE

THE JATAKA TALES: A DEEPER LOOK INTO THE TEACHINGS OF BUDDHISM THROUGH THESE ANCIENT STORIES

Jataka Tales are collections of ancient animal fables from India, traditionally centered around the teachings of Buddhism. These traditional stories date back centuries, and were passed down orally from generation to generation. While containing elements from various cultures, the foundation of these stories remains faithful to the core teachings of Buddhism, such as the notion of samsara, reincarnation, and the path to enlightenment.

The main content of the Jataka Tales revolves around the Buddha himself. He makes appearances in the majority of the stories as either an animal or a deity, and the tales revolve around his past life as a Bodhisattva, or an enlightened being. Through these stories, Buddhist principles of righteous behavior, kindness and consideration, and non-attachment to the material world are exemplified and taught. In many stories those who are portrayed with falling victim to the temptations of power or wealth are ascribed punishments that serve as warnings to those who may be tempted to act greedily.

In addition to their moral aspects, the stories of the Jataka Tales also serve to teach an understanding of karma, the spiritual law of cause and effect. Much like the stories of Cinderella or Beauty and The Beast, the characters in these tales are often observed taking actions which reap consequences, whether good or bad. In this way, these stories tend to be quite effective in teaching the audience about the consequences of their actions and the importance of living with kindness and integrity.

The teachings of such tales are often illustrated through the use of colorful and vivid characters, encompassing a wide range of animals from tigers and lions to even monkeys and hares. In many cases, the physical qualities of these animals are equated with human traits, providing the audience with an allegorical view of the stories.

The Jataka collection of animal stories have played an important role in spreading Buddhist philosophy. By presenting stories of right and wrong in a vivid and interesting fashion, these stories have been able to captivate their audience for centuries, helping to explain not only Buddhist principles but also a holistic view of ethical behavior. From tales of courageous kings to heartfelt stories of friendship, these ancient works of literature remain as relevant and meaningful today as they were centuries ago.

"India is a land of many wonders, a land of many contrasts, a land of many mysteries." - Paul Theroux

TEN

THE LEGENDS OF THE INDIAN GODS: UNDERSTANDING THE SYMBOLISM AND DEEPER MEANINGS IN THE STORIES OF THE HINDU GODS AND GODDESSES

The Hindu pantheon is filled with vibrant gods and goddesses, each one representing a variety of symbols, themes and values. Indian gods and goddesses, often collectively referred to as "legends", have long been an integral part of the country's history, culture and religious beliefs.

The gods and goddesses of Indian legends are complex and multi-layered, each with its own unique set of stories and symbolic meanings. They often represent basic elements of nature, such as fire, water, storms and other natural phenomena. Many gods and goddesses also embody abstract concepts, such as peace, justice and wisdom.

One of the most well-known figures from Indian mythology is Lord Shiva. Shiva is usually portrayed with blue skin and four arms, signifying his multitasking nature. He often is depicted as a fierce warrior riding a white bull named Nandi, which symbolizes his strength and power. Shiva is typically regarded as the god of destruction, with the power to create and transform. Other legends associate him with creation, and he is often considered to be the god of yoga.

The great mother goddess, Shakti, is known for her tenacious spirit and ability to defeat darkness. Shakti is usually represented as a beautiful woman with multiple arms, representing her ability to perform multiple tasks at once. Many Hindus believe that Shakti is the energy that powers the universe. She is associated with creation, destruction, light and growth.

Ganesha is another beloved figure in Indian culture.

Ganesha is the god of success and is typically portrayed with an elephant's head. His rat (or occasionally mouse) symbolizes intelligence, while his curved trunk conveys wisdom and knowledge. He is immensely popular and is seen as a source of luck during important events and ceremonies.

Goddess Saraswati is associated with intelligence, culture, knowledge and wisdom. She is the patroness of learning and is shown riding a white swan, which is symbolic of purity. She is usually depicted with four arms, each one of which holds a sacred object. The objects in her hands, such as a prayer book, lotus, rosary and vina, each carry their own special meaning.

Thus, the legends of gods and goddesses from the Indian subcontinent are full of symbolism and carry potent meanings. These gods and goddesses help to form a collective identity for the country, reflecting its values and culture. As such, they serve as positive role models for those who practice the Hindu faith.

ppp

"India is a land of ancient wisdom, where tradition and modernity coexist in perfect harmony." - J.K. Rowling

ELEVEN

THE FOLKTALES OF INDIA: UNDERSTANDING THE CULTURAL AND SPIRITUAL SIGNIFICANCE OF THESE STORIES AND THE MESSAGES THEY CONVEY

Folktales India is a source of Indian traditional values and expressions of folk culture. Stories of wisdom, heroism, adventure, romance and morality play an important role in imparting essential life lessons and values to the younger generations. The stories are used as moral guidance and serve as a mode of spiritual guidance.

Folktales act as a tool for the preservation of native Indian practices and culture. In India, stories are told to pass on knowledge and values from one generation to the next. Through these tales, people learn about family, community, culture and customs which have been passed down from old times. It is also a way for people to connect with their past as the stories reveal their place of origin and ancestry.

The stories also have a spiritual significance for many. Generally, the theme of the story is that of an individual's journey to spiritual enlightenment. In most cases, the characters are on a quest and have gone through trials and difficulties. By listening to the stories and reflecting on their meaning, people learn to develop inner strength and courage to face difficult situations in life.

The stories of India also bring life lessons to the young. The stories help children and young adults to develop a sense of right and wrong, as well to gain insights into the spiritual realm. The stories also help them to understand the consequences of their actions and the right choices to make in life.

The stories of India also have strong historical and cultural significances. They act as a source of inspiration and teach people to remain connected with the values and practices of the past. The stories help people to recognize the change, evolution and development of the Indian culture and traditions.

Folktales are a highly significant part of Indian culture, spirituality, and history. It serves as an effective way to keep the customs and culture of Indian alive in the hearts of all generations. By listening to and reflecting on the stories, people gain spiritual guidance, insights into the past cultures and traditions, and life lessons.

ʕʕʕ

Other Books Of The Author

1. The Moments When I Met God
2. Kashiyile Theertha Pathangal
3. GURU GYAN VANI
4. Abhiprerak Gita
5. ASSI SE JAIN GHAT TAK
6. Hopelessness of Arjuna
7. The Soul and It's True Nature
8. Sense of Action (Karma)
9. Action through Wisdom
10. Action through Wisdom
11. THEORY AND PRACTICAL OF EVERY ACTION
12. LOGICAL UNDERSTANDING OF THE SUPREME
13. THE IMPERISHABLE SUPREME
14. Yatra Nishadraj se Hanuman Ghat Tak
15. Yatra Karnatak Ghat se Raja Ghat Tak
16. Yatra Pandey Ghat se Prayagraj Ghat Tak
17. Yatra Ranjendra Prasad Ghat se Dattatreya Ghat Tak
18. YaatraSindhiya Ghat se Gwaliar Ghat Tak
19. Yatra Mangala Gauri Ghat se Hanuman Gadhi Ghat Tak
20. Yatra Gaay Ghat Se Nishad Ghat Tak
21. MAA GANGA, GHATEN EVM UTSAV
22. Ganga Arti Dev Deepavali evam Any Utsav
23. Potentials of Digitalized India
24. VEDIC CONSCIOUSNESS
25. A Brief Introduction to Vedic Science
26. Kashi ke Barah Jyotirling
27. IMPACT OF MOTIVATION
28. Let's have a Milky Way Journey
29. Color Therapy in a Nutshell

59. The Holistic Cow: A Look at the Physical, Spiritual, and Cultural Importance of Cows in India
60. Arts of Healing
61. Exploring the Divine
62. Understanding Five Elements
63. The Etymology of Ram
64. Symbols of India
65. Voice of Change (About Speeches of Great Men)
66. She Speaks (About Speeches of Great Women)
67. **Patriotism on Celluloid – Brief About Patriotic Films**
68. **The Music of Motivation: A Brief Guide to Inspirational Film Songs**
69. **Unlocking the Secrets of the Dashopanishads**

A CULTURAL MOSAIC
Ancient Traditions, Modern Minds
Beneath the Surface

Dr. Jagadeesh Pillai is a renowned Guinness World Record holder, writer, and researcher hailing from Varanasi, also known as the abode of Lord Shiva. With a Ph.D. in Vedic Science and a range of creative ideas and achievements, he is a true polymath. He is the author of more than 100 books including Research Publications. Although his roots can be traced back to Kerala, the people of Varanasi hold him in high regard and affectionately consider him one of their own.

Dr. Pillai has achieved four Guinness World Records in the following subjects:

"Script to Screen" - In this record, Dr. Pillai produced and directed an animation film within the shortest time possible, breaking the previous record set by Canadians. He has also received numerous national and international awards and recognitions for this achievement.

Longest Line of Postcards - For this record, Dr. Pillai created a line of 16,300 postcards on the occasion of the 163rd anniversary of Indian Postal Day. The event also included a questionnaire about the Indian flag.

Largest Poster Awareness Campaign - Dr. Pillai designed an awareness campaign on the subject of "Beti Bachao - Beti Padhao" (Save the Girl Child - Educate the Girl Child) to achieve this record.

Largest Envelope - In tribute to the Indian Prime Minister's "Make in India" initiative, Dr. Pillai created a 4000 square meter envelope using waste paper to achieve this record.

Attempted - **70000 Candles on a 210 kg Cake** - To celebrate the 70th Indian Independence Day, Dr. Pillai attempted to light 70,000 candles on a 210 kg cake, which was recorded in World Records India.

Attempted - **Documentary on Dhamek Stupa of Sarnath in 17 Languages** - Dr. Pillai attempted to create a documentary on the Dhamek Stupa of Sarnath, dubbing it in 17 different languages. The result of this attempt is currently awaiting confirmation from the Guinness World Records.

Dr. Pillai is skilled in teaching the Bhagavad Gita, a Hindu scripture, and is popular among young people. He has helped many young people improve their lives through his motivational teachings.

In addition to teaching, he has composed and sung numerous Sanskrit Bhajans and patriotic songs.

He has also written and directed several short films and documentaries for awareness campaigns, and has volunteered with the police in both UP and Kerala to spread awareness about various issues through videos and photography.

Incredibly, he has produced and directed over 100 documentaries about the city of Varanasi, all on his own.

He has also helped and guided more than 25 boys and girls to achieve world records through creative and innovative methods. He is a multifaceted person who uses his intellect and the blessings given to him by God to excel in various areas. He is both a teacher and a student, always learning and teaching, and is able to master any subject he comes across.

He is a selfless social activist and motivational speaker who has overcome struggles and failures to become a successful and enthusiastic individual with a rich life experience.

In addition to his work with the Bhagavad Gita, he is also an efficient Tarot card reader, Astro-Vastu consultant, and a talented singer and composer. He has sung the entire Ram Charita Manas and Bhagavad Gita in his own compositions, and has sung the phrase "Lokah Samastha Sukhino Bhavantu" in 50 different languages. He is currently working on a detailed and scientific study of Vedas, Upanishads, Puranas, and the Bhagavad Gita. He has also composed and sung the Hanuman Chalisa and Gayatri Mantra in 108 and 1008 different compositions, respectively.

Awards - Four Times Guinness World Records, Winner of Mahatma Gandhi Vishwa Shanti Puraskar, Mahatma Gandhi Global Peace Ambassador, Kashi Ratna Award, Dr. APJ Abdul Kalam Motivational Person of the Year 2017, Mother Teresa Award, Indira Gandhi Priyadarshini Award, Bharat Vikas Ratna Award, Udyog Ratna Award, Vigyan Prasar Award, Poorvanchal Ratn Samman.

Contact

DR. JAGADEESH PILLAI

PhD in Vedic Science

Four Times Guinness World Record Holder

Winner of Mahatma Gandhi Vishwa Shanti Puraskar and Global Peace Ambassador

Gemology, Astro & Vastu Consultant - Spiritual Counselor

Consultant for designing World Record Ideas

Efficient Tarot Card Reader

9839093003

myrichindia@gmail.com

drjagadeeshpillai@facebook

drjagadeeshpillai@instagram

jagadeeshpillai@youtube

www. JAGADEESHPILLAI.com

Reference

|| Internet, Various Scriptures & Libraries ||

|| LOKAHA SAMASTHAHA SUKHINO BHAVANTU ||

• 75 •